a guide to growing

fabulous fuchsias

a guide to growing

fabulous fuchsias

Blaise Cooke

LORENZ BOOKS

This edition first published by Lorenz Books

Lorenz Books is an imprint of Anness Publishing Limited
Hermes House, 88–89 Blackfriars Road, London SE1 8HA

Published in the USA by Lorenz Books
Anness Publishing Inc
27 West 20th Street, New York, NY 10011; (800) 354-9657

This edition distributed in Canada by Raincoast Books
8680 Cambie Street, Vancouver, British Columbia V6P 6M9

ISBN 0-7548-0551-4

A CIP catalogue record for this book is available from the British Library

Publisher: Joanna Lorenz
Project Editor: Fiona Eaton
Designer: Alan Marshall
Photographer: John Freeman
Additional photographers: Marie O'Hara, 69, 76-7;
Peter Anderson, 14-18, 43, 88-9; Peter McHoy. 45
Stylist: Bettina Graham
Contributor: Stephanie Donaldson, 69, 76-7

Jacket
Design and Art Direction: Clare Reynolds
Front cover image: Flowers & Foliage Picture Library/Karin Taylor

Previously published as *Step-by-Step Fabulous Fuchsias*

Printed and bound in China

1 3 5 7 9 10 8 6 4 2

Contents

Introduction

Visitors to any flower garden or show from early summer through to the autumn will surely be impressed by the colourful fuchsias. A mass of flowers can be produced on plants grown as bushes planted in beds or in pots, in baskets with strong upright or weeping growth or as tall standards, elegant on a patio or in a flower bed.

Fuchsias grow well alone or are suitable plants for mixing to produce a colourful summer display. The full blooms of cultivars with "double" flowers will add a richness to any group of flowering or foliage plants. The more simple, single-flowered plants producing a mass of flowers can make a lovely show.

Fuchsia plants are ideal for children to grow, rewarding any attention with colourful flowers. Dwarf fuchsias planted into bright pots will attract attention and may encourage your child to develop "green fingers".

The many fuchsia cultivars that now present a kaleidoscope of colour and form have been derived over many decades from the original species. Many of these species are still in cultivation and are becoming increasingly popular as their flowers have the appeal of elegance.

The ease with which fuchsia plants can be propagated and grown to flowering is a bonus for any gardener. Young shoots will root readily and quickly, so favourite cultivars can be shared and exchanged. Once established, plants will grow and flourish in almost all garden conditions.

For many people, growing fuchsias starts as an idle interest and develops into a rewarding passion. Happy growing!

The History of Fuchsias

Fuchsias were first introduced to Europe in the early eighteenth century in the form of a published botanical description. This was the work of a missionary, Father Plumier, who, in 1703, published a description of a plant he named *Fuchsia triphylla flore coccinea*, honouring a German professor of Botany, Leonard Fuchs, with the name. Unfortunately, the origin of the plant was not identified with the description and it was almost 100 years before fuchsia plants were collected again and made available for cultivation in Europe.

Following their introduction, fuchsias rapidly gained popularity. They flourished because their heating requirements were less demanding than other exotics, and as garden plants they were popular for their long and generous flowering season.

Several of the species that were introduced early in the history of fuchsia cultivation have had a major impact on the cultivars available today. The first fuchsia, *F. triphylla*, originating from Haiti, is in fact extremely difficult to grow, so much so that it is now rarely seen in cultivation. As one of the parents of the popular "triphylla" group, which were raised in Germany at the end of the nineteenth century, however, it still has a prominent profile. *F. magellanica* and *F. coccinea*, both originating from the Southern Andes and the uplands of south-east Brazil, were also early introductions and were easily cultivated in Europe. Although both species have small flowers, they are tolerant of cool growing conditions, and have played a major role in the parenthood of the modern hardy cultivars.

Above: Fuchsia magellanica *var.* gracilis.
Left: A magnificent display of fuchsias creates a stunning feature in any garden.

Increasingly through the nineteenth century, colour became an important element in the garden, and bright displays were achieved through the use of bedding plants. Tender fuchsias, such as members of the "triphylla" group, planted out into summer bedding schemes must have contributed. In the late nineteenth century, double-flowered cultivars appeared, several of which are still grown.

Modern goals in fuchsia breeding include the development of ever larger flowers, and of course the search for the still elusive yellow fuchsia and blue flowers that do not fade to lilac.

Top: Fuchsia fulgens *was introduced from Mexico in the 1830s and was used for hybridization to develop many of the cultivars we know today.*
Above: Fuchsia baccicaris.
Right: A redoute of Fuchsia dependens *drawn in 1891.*

Species Fuchsias

The richly colourful flowering fuchsia plants grown today have all been produced from a small group of wild fuchsia species introduced to cultivation in Europe since the eighteenth century. Several of these species are very decorative plants and delightful to grow both for their own flowers and for interest in their breeding history.

Some understanding of their natural growing conditions can provide helpful information towards growing both these species plants and their cultivars. Fuchsia species occur as wild plants in the mountainous areas of South and Central America, New Zealand and Tahiti, where they grow in forest soils rich in leaf mould. Their roots spread through the rich surface layer of the soil, where nutrients and moisture are more freely available.

Above: Fuchsia arborescens.
Below left: Fuchsia magellanica.
Below right: Fuchsia paniculata.

Fuchsia magellanica* var. *pumila
F. magellanica and *F. coccinea* were among the first fuchsias to be grown in Europe. Naturalized banks of *F. magellanica* cover western Ireland and south-west Britain, where it is much used for hedging, the scarlet flowers glowing throughout the summer and early autumn months. These species are probably responsible for the hardiness of some fuchsia cultivars.

Fuchsia arborescens* and *Fuchsia paniculata
F. arborescens and *F. paniculata* are both often known as "Lilac fuchsia". Both species have numerous small flowers collected into large terminal clusters held above the lustrous foliage. The flowers of *F. arborescens* are delicately scented. These Mexican species both make interesting, large bushy conservatory plants.

Fuchsia boliviana
This species and *F. boliviana* var. *alba* are both classified as climbing shrubs. Both are tender conservatory shrubs with a vigorous but lax habit, large soft leaves and enormous clusters dripping with red flowers.

Fuchsia denticulata
F. denticulata, native to Peru and Bolivia, is a spreading, tender shrub that produces numerous suckers from the base. The stems bear dark leaves that have vivid orange-green flowers in their axils.

Fuchsia encliandra* ssp *encliandra* and *Fuchsia microphylla
F. encliandra ssp *encliandra* and *F. microphylla* belong to the "encliandra" group, which embraces several species mostly native to Central America. All of them have tiny, brilliant flowers (usually less than 1 cm (1/2 in)

Top left: Fuchsia denticulata.
Top right: Fuchsia microphylla.
Left: Fuchsia boliviana.
Above: Fuchsia encliandra *ssp* encliandra.

long) and small leaves. The growth is often wiry, making these fuchsias ideal for creative topiary or wire work. Several delightful cultivars have been developed from this group, including *F.* 'Lottie Hobby'. Many of the fuchsias in this group may prove hardy in temperate climates.

Above left: Fuchsia fulgens.
Above: Fuchsia splendens.
Right: Triphylla-type F. *'Thalia'*
Below: Fuchsia procumbens.

Fuchsia fulgens

F. fulgens and *F. fulgens* 'Rubra Grandiflora' produce vermilion flowers that are up to 10 cm (4 in) long, held against soft, pale green foliage. Both the species and the variety 'Rubra Grandiflora' are easy to grow and make rewarding container or tub conservatory plants. *F. fulgens* was one of the important parents of what are known as the "triphylla" hybrids, all of which have strikingly long flower tubes.

Fuchsia procumbens

F. procumbens grows well in sandy soils that reflect its native littoral habitat in New Zealand. This species produces trailing shoots that will root and it can be used as a ground cover plant. The flowers are small, yellow-green with strikingly blue pollen. A closely allied fuchsia, *F. excorticata,* also from New Zealand, forms small trees in its native land.

Fuchsia splendens

This species from Central America, crossed with *F. triphylla* and *F. fulgens*, was an early parent of the "triphylla" hybrids. The sepals have a green tinge that is a feature of some of the progeny, such as *F.* 'Börnemanns Beste'.

Fuchsia triphylla

F. triphylla, originating from Haiti, is extremely difficult to grow, and so rarely seen in cultivation. It has dark green-bronze foliage that is now a characteristic of the "triphylla" hybrids. Varieties of this group are usually tender, with luxuriant panicles of long-tubed flowers glowing against their velvety leaves. 'Mary' was one of the first "triphylla" cultivars developed.

Fuchsia Flowers

In catalogues and nursery descriptions, fuchsia plants are usually described with reference to the form of their flowers: single, semi-double, double or triphylla-type. Since they were first introduced over two hundred years ago, growers have been crossing and re-crossing fuchsias. The simple flowers of wild species have been bred into more complex semi-double and double flowers.

Fuchsia flowers can be entirely one colour or different sections of the flower can be different colours. As fuchsia plants are usually grown for their flowers, these sections are described individually as the *tube,* the *sepals* and the *corolla.*

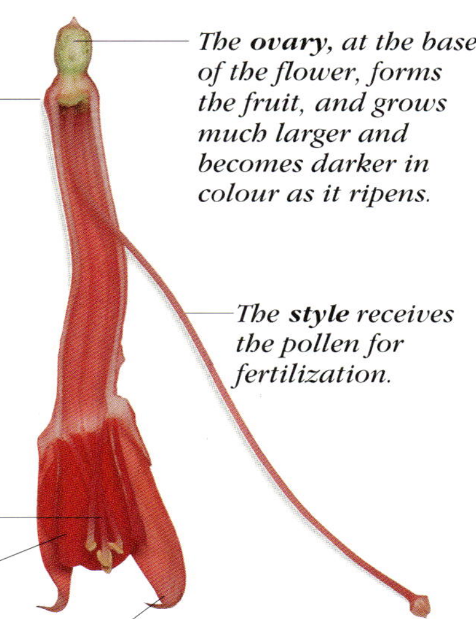

*The **tube** is the lower part of the flower, fixed to the ovary. Long tubes occur particularly in species fuchsias and in triphylla-type flowers. In the wild, fuchsias are pollinated by hummingbirds that have tongues long enough to sip the nectar released from special glands at the base of the fuchsia tube.*

*The **stamens** carry pollen in the terminal anthers.*

*The **corolla** is another term for the petals.*

*The **ovary**, at the base of the flower, forms the fruit, and grows much larger and becomes darker in colour as it ripens.*

*The **style** receives the pollen for fertilization.*

*The **sepals** enclose the flower when it is in bud. As the flower opens, they flare out from the top of the tube and are usually of the same colour. There are usually four sepals (rarely five).*

• Single flowers have four or rarely five petals. This sort of flower is often known as a "magellanica" type after the species *Fuchsia magellanica.* The single flower form reflects the closeness of these cultivars to the original species.

• Semi-double flowers have between five and seven petals.

• Double flowers have more than eight petals.

• Triphylla-type flowers are usually very long and tend to be red-orange.

Choosing Fuchsias

Before you decide which fuchsias to grow, you need to consider where you are going to grow them. Are they going to be planted in summer containers or baskets, or in your flower beds to enjoy year after year? Are beautiful flowers the most important consideration, or will the plants be valued for their foliage, too?

As with all plants, there is some overlap between the different types of fuchsia and plenty of room for personal preferences in colour and shape, but whichever type you choose, you are sure to be rewarded with beautiful blooms and a very colourful summer.

Varieties for pots and tubs
Most fuchsias will thrive in containers, but the most suitable are the bush, or upright, varieties. An upright fuchsia will give height and impact, creating a focal point for the display. Cultivars to try include: 'Pink Fantasia', 'Army Nurse' and 'Celia Smedley'. Uprights with an arching habit – where the weight of the flowers pulls the stems downwards – look good if they tumble over the edges of pots. 'Brutus', 'Dark Eyes' and 'Annabel' are good examples.

Fuchsias for hanging baskets and window boxes
Many fuchsia varieties grow with cascades of beautifully formed flowers hanging down in abundance from the stems – these varieties can be displayed to their best advantage in hanging baskets, where the flowers are seen from below. Trailing varieties, with their vine-like stems, are ideally suited to hanging basket arrangements – try *Fuchsia* 'Autumnale' which has glorious bronze foliage, *Fuchsia* 'Harry Gray', and *Fuchsia* 'La Campanella' with semi-double mauve and white blooms. Some of the upright varieties can also be used for hanging baskets, particularly if they have full flowers that will pull the stems down with them, over the sides of the basket; for example *Fuchsia* 'Flying Cloud' and *Fuchsia* 'Annabel'.

Far left: Fuchsia *'Pink Fantasia' is a half-hardy fuchsia that holds its flowers erect from the plant, making it ideal for pots and beds. The single flowers have dark purple corollas veined with pink and pink sepals.*
Left: Fuchsia *'Army Nurse', a hardy fuchsia, can be grown in a container and is suitable for training as a standard. The small semi-double flowers have blue-violet corollas and deep carmine-red sepals.*

Standards
Standard fuchsias are increasingly popular as they provide a stunning centrepiece for flower beds and large containers. Training a standard fuchsia takes time and patience, but your efforts will be well rewarded. You will have your own preference for the colour and type of standard you want, and virtually any fuchsia can be used. *Fuchsia* 'Celia Smedley' and 'Cotton Candy' are both suitable cultivars for training into fine standards.

Left: Fuchsia *'Grandma Sinton' is suitable for hanging baskets and would make a lovely weeping standard.*
Bottom left: Fuchsia *'Celia Smedley' is a vigorous plant with an upright habit.*
Bottom right: Double-flowered Fuchsia *'Cotton Candy' is an upright plant that makes a good standard.*

Growing hardy fuchsias
A number of fuchsias are hardy enough to survive winter weather and so make excellent plants for adding height and interest to herbaceous borders. In some milder areas the top growth will survive; in sustained colder temperatures the shrub will die down to ground level. If you cut off the dead top growth in spring the plants will produce new shoots. *Fuchsia* 'Alice Hoffman', *Fuchsia* 'Genii' and *Fuchsia* 'Tom Thumb' are all hardy cultivars that would make a colourful impression in the borders in your garden.

Left: Fuchsia *'Alice Hoffman' is a compact upright plant that grows particularly well in containers.*
Above: Fuchsia *'Tom Thumb' is a hardy cultivar with a compact, bushy shape. It is suitable for rock gardens and may also be trained as a miniature standard.*

Fuchsias for foliage
Fuchsias offer such a wealth of beautiful flowers that it can be quite easy to overlook the many wonderful shades of foliage in the fuchsia spectrum. 'Eden Princess', 'Golden Eden Lady', 'Popsie Girl', 'Thalia' and 'Cloth of Gold' are all worth growing simply for their unusual leaf colouring, but better still, the flowers are equally appealing.

Below: Fuchsia *'Golden Eden Lady'.*
Right: Fuchsia *'Eden Princess'.*
Far right: Fuchsia *'Genii'.*

Fuchsias as Bedding Plants

An eye-catching summer display can be created using the strong colours and continuous flower production of a selection of fuchsias. The enormous variety in flower colour and form can be the basis of a planting scheme, or plants can be used in smaller groups to fill any available garden space between permanent flowering plants or as spot colour in a leafy border.

Gardener's Tip

A little soil preparation prior to planting will ensure good growth of the plants. Dig over the planting site with a spade to loosen the soil and to check that there is reasonable drainage. A light dressing of fertilizer or bonemeal, following the manufacturer's recommended dosage, should be sprinkled on the surface and then raked in.

Opposite: In this garden setting, a mixture of fuchsia cultivars and other herbaceous plants have been grouped to create a stunning, colourful effect.

Arrange the fuchsia plants in odd-numbered blocks of 3 or 5 of the same cultivar. Group plantings of odd numbers of the same cultivar will give the display the most impact. Use the wide variety of colours available for contrast, and try to avoid planting blocks of similarly coloured fuchsias too closely.

When you design a planting scheme, consider the features of the plants such as flower and foliage colour as well as height. Dwarf or low-growing plants should be used in the front of a border, and the taller varieties further back. Standard fuchsias can be used effectively to give extra height in a border, although these must be well staked to avoid wind damage.

Fuchsia bedding will thrive best in a slightly shaded position where the flowers and foliage are not scorched by the summer sun. Regular watering is vital, particularly for freshly planted fuchsias as the roots will not have had time to establish a strong root-run. To encourage continuous flowering and strong growth, feed the plants once a week using a balanced fertilizer.

Plant bedding fuchsias in the garden in early summer, once all danger of a late frost is past.

Above: 'Charming' is a hardy bedding fuchsia. It was introduced in 1889, and is one of the oldest cultivars still generally available.

Above: 'Lord Lonsdale' is a half-hardy bedding fuchsia. Its unique flowers have salmon-orange corollas and apricot-pink sepals tipped with green.

Conservatory Fuchsias

To grow fuchsias indoors it helps to consider the conditions in which they would be growing in their native environment. Most of the species occur in the heavily humid forests growing on the slopes of mountains in South America. Here the air is moist and the plants are shaded. This is in direct contrast to the conditions in which most plants are grown indoors.

In a conservatory where a humid atmosphere can be maintained by spraying water liberally over the plants, fuchsias will thrive.

On windowsills and elsewhere indoors, a humid microclimate can be achieved around the plants if they are placed on saucers containing expanded clay granules or pebbles. Do not allow the base of the pot to be submerged or constantly wet, but use the granules to lift the plant just above the water. Regular misting will reduce the susceptibility of the shoot tips to drying and will also reduce the dropping of flower buds.

Where the light comes from one direction, the plants must be regularly turned. Give each plant a quarter turn daily to prevent the growth becoming very lop-sided. Fuchsias that produce short stems and have a compact growth habit will be the most successful for conservatory cultivation. Less compact plants will tend to become leggy and unattractive.

Right: 'Snowfire' was introduced in 1978. The pretty double flowers have bright pink to coral-red corollas and white sepals.

Recommended cultivars
'Bambini'
'Dollar Princess'
'Heidi Ann'
'Helen Clare'
'Nellie Nuttall'
'Snowfire'
'String of Pearls'
'Waveney Gem'

Opposite: Decorative plant stands will display flowering plants to advantage in a conservatory, so that they become focal points against a background of foliage.

GARDENER'S TIP

Young plants will become conditioned to the conservatory environment more rapidly and become established and grow better than older plants.

Nursery Plants

Fuchsia plants are available from nurseries in several different forms. Individual plants can be bought in small pots, or several plants, intended for use as bedding plants, can be purchased in polystyrene trays. Nursery plants are usually available from early spring through to the early summer months.

MATERIALS AND TOOLS
Potting compost (soil mix)
Plastic pots 7.5 cm (3 in) diameter
Watering can

PLANTS
Individual fuchsia plants in small pots, or in polystyrene trays

young fuchsia plants

1 Break open the polystyrene tray to expose the rootball. Gently lift the plants from the tray.

2 Place a little compost (soil mix) in the base of a plastic pot.

3 Position the young plant in the fresh pot so that the surface of the rootball is below the rim of the pot. Trickle compost around the rootball and firm it into place with your fingers. Be careful not to compress the compost too solidly. Water the plant.

GARDENER'S TIP

Check the base of the pots or the tray for visible and vigorous roots before you buy the plants.

Mail Order Plants

Ordering fuchsias through the post may be necessary for special or choice varieties or when a visit to a nursery is not possible. The young plants are mailed in special packages that minimize damage during transit, but as the plants are restricted and in the dark for a while, they are initially weakened; care is necessary to encourage them into vigorous growth.

Materials and Tools
Potting compost (soil mix)
Plastic pots 7.5 cm (3 in) diameter
Watering can

Plants
Mail order fuchsias

young fuchsia plants

1 Open the package with care. Leaves will probably unfold from the confined space. Each plant should be intact and clearly labelled.

2 Lift the plants out of the package. Labels tucked underneath the rootball reduce the necessity for handling it and so keep the compost (soil mix) intact.

3 Position the young plant on a shallow layer of compost in a plastic pot. Add compost and firm it around the rootball to fill all the gaps.

4 If the plants appear to be very wilted or stressed, remove some of the larger leaves carefully with your finger and thumb. Water the plants using a watering can fitted with a fine rose for a gentle spray.

Gardener's Tip

Take care not to lose or muddle the labels on new plants. Label plants with plastic, indelible labels as soon as possible.

Plants from Seed

Fuchsia seeds can be collected from ripe fruits and cleaned, or purchased. They should be sown as soon as possible. The resulting plants are usually new cultivars and may be very interesting or may be extremely disappointing.

Materials and Tools
Plastic tray of cells
Scissors
Seed compost (soil mix)
Seeds
Sieve
Horticultural sand
Watering can with fine rose
Large clear jar with screw top

fuchsia seeds

1 Trim the plastic tray of cells so that it fits through the neck of the jar. Fill the tray with seed compost (soil mix) and firm with a smaller section of the tray.

2 Put up to three seeds on to the surface of the compost in each cell close to the centre, but spaced so that you can remove weaker seedlings later.

3 Using the sieve, sprinkle a thin layer of sand over the seeds.

4 Gently water the cells using a watering can with a fine rose. Put the tray into the jar and screw on the top. Leave the jar in a shaded location with a stable temperature of between 18–21°C (65–70°F). Germination should be rapid, with the first seedlings appearing within 2 weeks.

5 After 3 months inside the closed jar, most of the seeds will have germinated. These seedlings have not yet developed their first pair of true leaves. Wait for the first true leaves before you thin out the weaker seedlings to leave only one seedling per cell.

Gardener's Tip

Do not be too quick to discard the compost (soil mix) in which you have sown the seeds. Fuchsia seeds have irregular germination and more seedlings may appear later. Interestingly, it has often been noted that these late germinations produce the nicest plants.

Hybridizing Plants

Producing new plants from your own seed is a gamble for a very rare winner but if you strike lucky it can be very worthwhile. There are over 10,000 fuchsia cultivars already and several intensive breeding programmes that are seeking elusive goals such as a yellow fuchsia flower or blue flowers that do not fade to lilac. Increasingly large and full double flowers are also a breeder's goal. If you feel inspired, try to cross-pollinate your favourite flowers and grow some of the resulting seedlings to flowering.

MATERIALS AND TOOLS
Scissors
Clean plastic bag
Plastic-coated wire ties

PLANTS
Flowering plants

flower before opening

1 Open a young flower bud by gently squeezing it between your fingers. It is important that you choose a bud that is still firmly closed, so that the female style is isolated from chance pollination.

2 Under the gentle pressure, the flower will open and the style and the stamens will unfurl. Using fine scissors, snip out all eight stamens. These are the pollen-bearing organs and if you miss one, the flower will be able to self-pollinate.

3 Isolate the treated flower in a plastic bag secured with a wire tie until the female style becomes receptive to pollen. The receptive state is indicated by the tip of the style becoming sticky.

4 Gently brush the flower chosen to be the pollen donor across the receptive style. You can isolate the pollinated female flower again afterwards to prevent further pollen deposition. Keep a clear note of the two cultivars used and the date of pollination. The production of ripe fruits will take several weeks.

GARDENER'S TIP

When the ripe fruits resemble small cherries, remove them from the plant and slit them open carefully on white kitchen paper. Inside will be a mass of small seeds either side of a central axis. These can be flicked out using a sharp cocktail stick. Not all the seeds will be viable. Viable seeds are usually larger and darker than the others and they sink when placed in water.

Taking Fuchsia Cuttings

Growing plants from cuttings opens the possibilities of safeguarding your favourite varieties and adding new plants for little cost. Cuttings almost always give rise to replicas of the parent plant. Occasionally, a branch may develop different characteristics from the rest of the plant, for example, a more intense variegation or leaves of a different colour. By taking cuttings off the branch, these changes can be captured and grown on in whole plants.

MATERIALS AND TOOLS
- Block of florist's foam 15 x 30 cm (6 x 12 in) or plastic pots and cuttings compost (soil mix)
- Sharp kitchen knife
- Seed tray
- Secateurs (pruners)
- Horticultural knife or sharp penknife
- Chopping board
- Fine stick
- Large, clear jar or plastic bag and elastic band
- Sprayer

fuchsia for cuttings

1 Prepare the materials for rooting the cuttings before you start to work with the plant material. Cut halfway through the block of florist's foam (if using) to divide it into small sections.

GARDENER'S TIP

Good cutting material should be healthy and vigorous. Choose material that has paired leaves of equal size. To grow a standard, use stems with three leaves arising from each node.

2 Soak the cut florist's foam sections. If you are using plastic pots and cuttings compost (soil mix), fill the pots and water them until they are thoroughly wet.

3 When you are ready, remove a piece of healthy, non-flowering growth from the fuchsia. Cut the branch cleanly with sharp secateurs (pruners). Do not leave the cut branch for long: it will dry rapidly and be less liable to form roots.

4 Using a sharp knife or penknife, cut the branch into sections. The best cutting is the growing tip, which should be cut so that it has one half-extended pair of leaves, one fully extended pair and a section of leafless stem 1.5 cm ($\frac{5}{8}$ in) long. The rest of the material can be divided into small cuttings, each with a fully extended pair of leaves above a short stem section. If the leaves are very large, you can reduce their area by cutting them in half.

5 Use the fine stick to make a hole in the centre of each foam section and gently push a cutting into each hole, taking care not to bruise the stem.

6 Once all the sections have been fitted with cuttings, insert the foam into a large, wide-necked clear glass or plastic jar. Screw on the lid of the jar.

7 Leave the enclosed cuttings in a light but not directly sunlit position. The optimum conditions for rooting fuchsia cuttings are a temperature of approximately 15°C (60°F) and a humid, still environment.

ALTERNATIVE METHOD

1 If using plastic pots, push the cuttings into the compost (soil mix) after making a hole for each one using the stick.

2 If you wish to grow a bushy plant, put up to seven cuttings around the edge of a larger pot. Each cutting should be at least 4 cm (1½ in) from its neighbour. Use a sprayer to settle the cuttings in the rooting medium. To decrease the dangers of the cuttings becoming infected with a fungal rot, use a diluted solution of fungicide instead of plain water.

3 Enclose the potted cuttings in a clear plastic bag, drawn tightly around the lip of the pot with an elastic band.

Hanging Baskets

A variety of hanging baskets are now available to suit different conditions and gardening requirements. The position for which the basket is intended will influence the type of basket that you choose for your planting.

Wire baskets usually have detachable chains that can be removed or set to one side while you plant the basket.

Baskets lined with sphagnum moss can be planted to create a complete, flowering ball of colour, with plants set in the top of the basket as well as through the moss lining. Such baskets require regular care and attention and sufficient room for growth.

Basket liners made from coconut coir, hessian (burlap) or other fibre can be substituted for moss. Purpose-cut liners can be purchased from most garden centres.

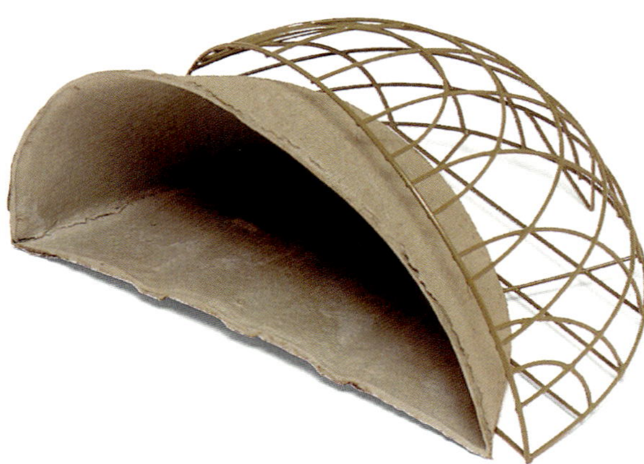

Cardboard liners are available in various sizes, and are also available for half-baskets. Some liners will have pre-punched holes that can be pushed out if you wish to use them for side planting.

Where water dripping from a hanging basket may cause problems, use one with a purpose-built reservoir. These baskets can look very decorative when the plants have grown sufficiently.

GARDENER'S TIP

The compost (soil mix) in a hanging basket is particularly prone to drying out. Use water-retaining gel or granules mixed into the compost to reduce the water stress to which the plants may be exposed.

Planting in Pots and Tubs

Planting in pots and tubs can offer the opportunity of creating miniature gardens, each with their own character, plant or colour theme. Before you arrange the plants, consider their growth needs, particularly their roots, and choose the container with care.

Planting in terracotta pots

The drainage through terracotta pots can be blocked if the hole in the base of the pot becomes obstructed by a solid mass of compost (soil mix). It is important to use broken crocks or brick fragments in the base of the pot to maintain the free drainage.

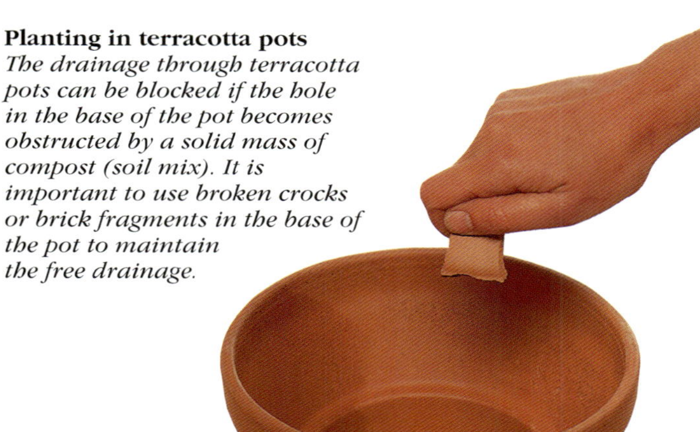

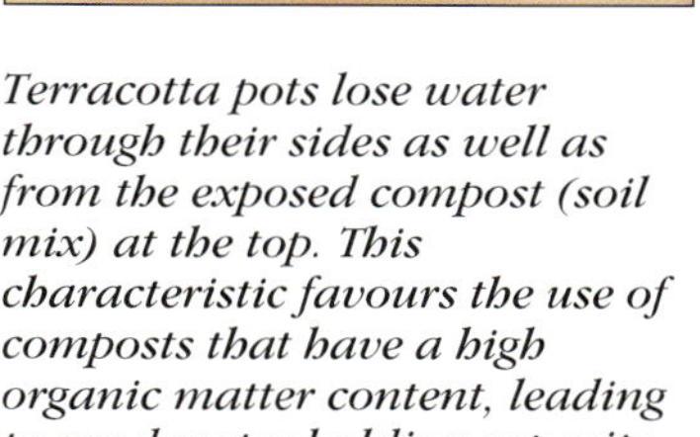

Terracotta pots lose water through their sides as well as from the exposed compost (soil mix) at the top. This characteristic favours the use of composts that have a high organic matter content, leading to good water-holding capacity.

Broken polystyrene plant trays in the base of large pots will reduce the amount of compost required for planting as well as reducing the weight of the container, which can be a benefit on roofs and balconies.

Planting in plastic pots

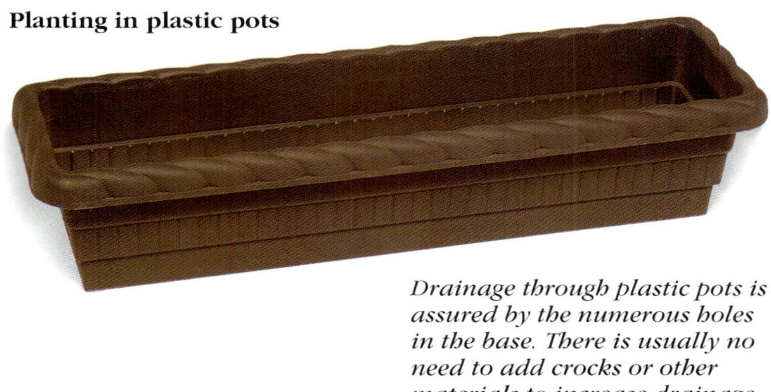

Drainage through plastic pots is assured by the numerous holes in the base. There is usually no need to add crocks or other materials to increase drainage.

Large plastic tubs can be robust containers suitable for a range of different plantings. Where the tub lacks drainage holes, sections of polystyrene plant trays in the bottom will lift the compost sufficiently to ensure adequate aeration and prevent waterlogging.

Composts (Soil Mixes) and Growing Media

Species fuchsias originate in the leaf litter layer of woods and forests, where nutrients and moisture are freely available. When you are growing fuchsias in pots, baskets or in the ground, remember their origins and provide your plants with growing conditions that have good drainage and nutrient levels.

Standard compost
The majority of composts available are peat-based with added fertilizers.

Peat-free compost
The organic content of these peat-free composts is derived from renewable sources such as coconut coir. Watch out for watering difficulties if you allow it to become too dry.

Loam-based compost
This compost is based upon sieved and sterilized loam, with added grit and some fertilizer. It resembles normal soil and is suitable for tubs and containers. Increase the organic content and the water-holding capacity by adding peat-free compost which will also reduce the weight.

Peat-based compost
The organic content in many composts is peat, which is light in weight. This compost holds water well, but is almost impossible to re-wet if it dries out and shrinks.

Vermiculite
Vermiculite, a matrix material shown here mixed with standard compost, will reduce the weight and increase the water-holding capacity of the compost mix.

Feeding Fuchsias

Regular feeding throughout the year will have an important impact on growth and flower production.

Always follow the guidelines presented on the product and never apply a stronger mix than is recommended. Be cautious when applying foliar feeds which, in strong sunlight, can cause scorching.

Liquid fertilizers (*above left*) are widely used. They can be applied through a watering can on to compost (soil mix) or where directed, as a foliar feed through the plant sprayer.

Feeding pellets (*centre*) composed of slow-release plant food granules are intended to release fertilizer into the compost continuously. Large pots or baskets may need more than one pellet.

Slow-release plant food granules (*right*) can be added to the compost or potting mix in the recommended quantity, using a spoon or scoop. These granules will release nutrients throughout the growing season.

Water-retaining additives
Matured organic matter (*above left*) can be added to potting composts to increase the water retention capacity.

Fragments of bark (*centre*) are used as a surface mulch. Mulching has an important impact on reducing water loss due to evaporation from the soil or compost.

Water-retaining gel (*right*) can be added to compost in granular form or pre-wetted into a gel. It is a valuable material to add to any containers such as baskets, pots or window boxes.

Watering Fuchsias

Watering solitary or grouped fuchsia plants requires careful and individual attention. Some plants will require a lot of water and others much less. Too much water is as bad as too little.

Watering can
A large watering can with a detachable rose is useful for watering large containers, pots and baskets. The fine spray produced by the rose is useful for trays for seeds and cuttings. The small can is helpful for watering single plants, especially those growing indoors.

Hand sprayer
Regular use of a hand sprayer will help to create a humid atmosphere for plants grown indoors. Some fertilizers can be applied as foliar feeds through the spray.

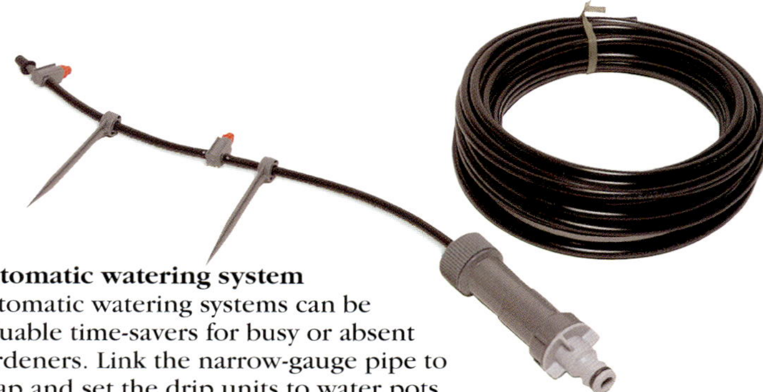

Automatic watering system
Automatic watering systems can be valuable time-savers for busy or absent gardeners. Link the narrow-gauge pipe to a tap and set the drip units to water pots, baskets, window boxes and even individual plants in a border. A timer can be fitted so that watering is switched on and off automatically.

Potting-on Young Plants

Young cuttings produce roots and start to grow very rapidly. Usually, young plants are sufficiently well rooted and ready for potting-on approximately one month after taking the cuttings. They will have grown an average of two sets of leaves at this stage.

Materials and Tools
Potting compost (soil mix)
Plastic pot 7.5 cm (3 in) diameter
Short, thin cane

Plants
Rooted cutting in 4 cm (1½ in) pot

fuchsia cutting

1 Remove the rooted cutting from its small pot. Check that the plant really is well rooted and that the roots are looking healthy.

2 Put a thin layer of compost (soil mix) into the larger pot and sit the rootball of the young plant on to it. Make sure that the surface of the rootball is below the lip of the pot, adjusting the amount of compost in the pot if necessary.

3 Hold the plant steady with one hand and ease fresh potting compost around the rootball.

4 Using the thin cane, gently push the compost down between the sides of the pot and the rootball.

Gardener's Tip

When potting-on young plants, move them into pots only one size larger than their rootball. If you put plants into pots that are too big, you risk rotting the roots due to their being surrounded by too large a mass of moist compost (soil mix).

Potting-back or Root-pruning

If you are growing a fuchsia for a special position or in a decorative container, you may wish to keep it in the same size pot year after year. Without fresh soil and root-pruning the plant will rapidly become pot-bound and the foliage will yellow. The revitalizing effect of root-pruning can be achieved through drastic removal of the old soil around the roots, or by using a sharp knife to cut away the bottom of the rootball.

MATERIALS AND TOOLS
Sharp secateurs (pruners)
Nail or short, thin cane
Compost (soil mix) with slow-release plant food
Sharp knife

PLANTS
Mature fuchsia plant

mature plant

1 Prune the stems and branches with secateurs (pruners). This reduction in top growth will decrease the strain on the disturbed root system. Hard pruning will also provide an opportunity to correct any poor growth form.

2 Using the nail or cane, tease the old compost (soil mix) away from the roots. Do not shrink from removing a substantial amount of the soil, as all fuchsias replace their roots very quickly.

3 Using the secateurs, prune away the exposed roots so that the root system is reduced by almost one-third. Make sure that you cut the roots cleanly without tearing them.

4 Add a layer of fresh compost to the bottom of the pot and reseat the reduced rootball slightly lower than it was initially. Add a shallow dressing of compost to the top of the pot to encourage new shoots to arise from the base of the plant.

GARDENER'S TIP

This procedure should be carried out during a natural pause in the flowering of the fuchsia. If you root-prune a plant in full flower, it is likely that the flowers will drop off.

ALTERNATIVE METHOD

1 Using a sharp knife, cut away a section of compost and roots from the bottom of the rootball. A slice approximately 2.5 cm (1 in) can safely be removed from most plants.

2 Do not worry if you have cut through large, tough roots: they will regrow. Repot, adding fresh compost. Feeding roots are usually located near the soil surface, so a top dressing will also promote growth.

End-of-season Pruning

Fuchsia plants need a dormant period to maintain healthy growth. Cold winter weather naturally slows growth, plants stop flowering and lose their leaves, and tender plants growing in pots are ready for pruning before overwinter storage. In milder regions a dormant period can be encouraged by severe pruning.

Materials and Tools
Bucket
Secateurs (pruners)

Plants
Mature fuchsia in hanging basket

trailing fuchsia

1 Set the hanging basket into the top of a bucket so that you can work easily around it.

2 Examine the plant and check the branching arrangement carefully before you start to prune. Look for young, vigorous branches arising from near the base of the plant. Using sharp, clean secateurs (pruners) start to cut away the long, trailing stems.

Gardener's Tip

Leave the fuchsia in the same potting mix over winter. In the spring either repot with fresh compost (soil mix) or add a shallow layer of fresh compost to the surface, together with a dose of slow-release plant food granules.

3 Work around the basket. Remove or reduce most of the stems but leave the main branches long enough to hang over the sides of the basket, ready to shoot with next season's growth.

4 Remove any remaining leaves from the pruned stems. Pick out any leaf or flower debris remaining on the surface of the potting compost (soil mix). Dead material can harbour pests and fungal infections.

5 The pruned basket should be kept in a cool but frost-free location. The cut ends of the stems will bleed a clear liquid after pruning. This will soon stop as the tissue dries.

Preparing for Winter

Overwintering fuchsias will depend on the severity of the local climate. If frosts are rare, the fuchsia plants will require only a short dormant period to ensure continuing strong growth; if frosts and freezing temperatures are frequent, more careful preparations are necessary.

Gardener's Tips

Before you start preparations for winter, examine the plants to verify that they are free of pests and in good health.

Never let the plants dry out over the dormant season. The compost (soil mix) should be damp but not wet throughout the winter.

Materials and Tools
Secateurs (pruners)
Newspaper
Cardboard box

Plants
Mature, tender fuchsias

mature fuchsia

1 Using secateurs (pruners), prune away the top growth to leave a structure of woody stems that will be the basis for the next season's growth.

2 Put a layer of insulating material, for example crumpled newspaper, into the cardboard box to insulate the fuchsias from the bottom of the box.

3 Wrap a collar of paper around the remaining woody stems, and stand or lay the plant on the layer of insulating material.

4 Continue filling the box with pruned and prepared plants. Add more insulating material to the box as you go, so that the plants are well insulated from the sides of the box and from each other.

5 Close the box and store it in a frost-free place, where the temperature is stable and between 0–4°C (32–39°F).

Fuchsia Calendar

This brief calendar lists some of the tasks that you will need to undertake at different times of the year to ensure healthy plants.

Spring

- Remove tender plants from winter storage and examine the stems carefully. Scrape a small section of bark to check for green growth.

- Finish any pruning that was left undone in the autumn.
- Root-prune or repot plants.

- Check hardy plants for similar signs as well as for rot or damage to the crown.
- After all risk of frost is past, prune hardy plants down to two pairs of leaf buds.
- Examine any autumn cuttings that you have grown over the winter months.

Summer

- As early summer growth commences, start to shape your plants and use some of the soft, green shoots for cuttings. Remember to label the cuttings clearly as you take them.
- Maintain vigorous growth throughout the summer by careful potting and feeding. Fuchsias are big feeders, so follow recommendations on the fertilizer packets.

- As flowering continues, pick off old flowers and young fruits. If you leave fruits on the plants, flowering will be suppressed. Move pots of tender fuchsias outside for the summer, where they will benefit from fresh air and good light.

Autumn

- Fuchsias will continue to flower into the autumn months. Encourage flowering by feeding with a balanced feed. Continue to remove spent flowers and developing fruits.

- Take cuttings from prized plants in case of losses over winter. Select non-flowering shoots and water the cuttings with a fungicide, as the development of roots and growth may be slow.

Winter

- Prune back tender fuchsias to encourage a strong structure for the next growing season.

- Check all remaining stems for pests or infections. Use a combined insecticide/fungicide spray and allow it to dry on the branches before putting the plants into storage.

Pests and Diseases

Prevention is always better than cure. Check plants regularly for early signs of stress or infection. Healthy plants will better resist infections, so follow good watering and feeding regimes to encourage strong growth. Remove debris to reduce the hiding and breeding places of pests.

Red spider mite
These tiny mites are difficult to spot and they spread rapidly. Attacks can be recognized by the appearance of leaves which become dull-looking and silvery bronze on the underside, and soon wither and fall. Severe infestations are obvious from the fine webs that develop. The mites thrive in a hot, dry atmosphere and are a sure sign of poor growing conditions.

Deter infestations by spraying regularly with water. Isolate any infected plant: either destroy it or remove all the leaves and spray with a systemic insecticide. In glasshouses, the biological predator *Phytoseiulus persimimilis* is a successful means of control.

Vine weevils
Adult weevils damage only the leaves of plants, making crescent-shaped notches on the margins. Active from early spring, they each lay up to 1,500 eggs in the soil, and the larvae feed on roots from late summer onwards. Sudden wilting of plants is an indication of an infestation. Biological control is the best solution.

Whitefly
Whitefly is most obvious in the adult phase as small, white moth-like insects, which fly briefly when disturbed. Found on the undersides of the leaves, both adults and immature stages feed on sap. They excrete a sugar-rich "honeydew" that soon becomes mouldy and turns black. They are particularly damaging to greenhouse plants and are difficult to eradicate. Sticky sheets can be hung between the plants to trap whitefly, and these should be examined frequently. Infestations in greenhouses can be treated by biological control using a small wasp, *Encarsia formosa*, as a predator, or by an infective fungus. It is not possible to mix biological and chemical treatments. If insecticidal sprays are used, applications should be alternated, using at least two different sprays.

Other insect pests
Bees and wasps may damage the flowers with their feet, bruising the petals which then become brown-flecked and spoilt. To get at the nectar they often cut a hole in the flower tube. Screens across doors and vents will keep them out of greenhouses.

Capsid bugs are pests of fuchsias grown in garden beds. The bugs, which are nocturnal, look like large greenfly, usually green but often brown. Attacks are recognized by disfiguration of the growing tips which will then not flower. Conifers are the main host for capsid bugs, and these as well as the fuchsia plants can be treated with chemicals to relieve the problem.

Botrytis
A major fungal disease of fuchsias, *Botrytis* most often occurs in late winter or early spring when growth is slow and air circulation is reduced. Infection is easily recognized as grey, hair-like mould on soft stems, flowers and leaves.

Good hygiene and ventilation are effective in the prevention of this disease. Systemic fungicides can also be helpful, but treatments should be varied to avoid development of resistance.

Fuchsia rust
This is the most dreaded fungal disease of fuchsias and can easily develop on plants growing under stressful conditions. Infection appears as orange patches on the underside of the leaves. The rust spreads rapidly and can occur on greenhouse as well as outdoor fuchsias.

The rust fungus also occurs on willow-herbs (*Epilobium* spp), so take care to remove these plants from the vicinity.

Rust-infected leaves should be removed immediately and destroyed. Infection can be prevented by spraying at two-weekly intervals with a thiram or zineb-based fungicide.

Growing a Bush

The easiest and possibly the most common way of growing fuchsias is as a bush since this is their most natural shape.

PLANTS

Young plants such as *Fuchsia* 'Annabel', 'Pink Fantasia', 'Nellie Nuttall' or 'Tom Thumb'

young fuchsia

1 To encourage vigorous growth of a young, single-stemmed plant, pinch out the growing tip. Side shoots will be encouraged to grow and therefore give a bushy shape to the plant.

2 After pinching out once, the plant will produce a number of side shoots. Pinch out one of the growing tips again to encourage further growth.

3 Continue pinching out more of the growing tips until you have a vigorous and compact plant.

GARDENER'S TIP

To create a fuchsia plant with a symmetrical shape, turn it regularly. A fuchsia that is not turned may grow in a lop-sided manner towards the light source.

Growing a Standard

Almost any variety of fuchsia can be trained to grow as a standard. Fuchsias with lax, trailing growth form a standard with a lovely weeping head, while bush fuchsias can be grown into bushy, mop-head standards.

MATERIALS AND TOOLS
Cane
Plastic-coated wire ties or twine

PLANTS
Young, rooted fuchsia cutting

fuchsia cutting

1 Choose a cutting with a straight stem and upright growth. Remove any side shoots. Gently insert a cane into the compost (soil mix) as close to the stem of the plant as possible.

GARDENER'S TIP

When selecting a cutting to grow into a standard, try to choose one with three leaves arising at each node. These cuttings have three buds which can grow and so will make a much fuller head on the standard than a cutting with only two leaves at each node.

2 Using a wire tie, gently bring the stem towards the cane and tie it closely. Leave the stem leaves on the plant. Remove side shoots as they arise on the lower section of the stem, but leave the shoots arising from the top five sets of leaves as they will form the head of the standard.

3 When the young plant has reached the required height, pinch out the growing tip. This will encourage the growth of the five sets of side shoots left below the tip.

4 When the side shoots have each grown five sets of leaves, pinch out their growing tips. This will encourage the shoots to branch.

5 The full head on a standard is developed by regularly pinching out the growing tips on the branches. When the stem has become quite woody, remove the remaining large stem leaves. Continue to remove any shoots that may arise from the stem.

Growing a Hoop

The supple growth of many fuchsias makes them very suitable plants for growing into decorative shapes around wire supports. They can be trained into wonderful, simple shapes such as hoops and fans, or more complicated forms. It is important to select an appropriate fuchsia for the shape. Small flowers and small leaves are usually more suitable than cultivars with large, double flowers. Here, the delicate flowers and small leaves of *Fuchsia* 'Katrina Thompsen' make it an ideal subject for a simple hoop.

MATERIALS AND TOOLS
Potting compost (soil mix)
Plastic pot 18 cm (7 in) diameter
Plastic-coated green wire formed into a hoop
Plastic-coated wire ties

PLANTS
2 *Fuchsia* 'Katrina Thompsen' in 7.5 cm (3 in) pots

Fuchsia *'Katrina Thompsen'*

1 Put a layer of compost (soil mix) in the base of the larger pot.

2 Remove the plastic pots from the two young plants and set them side by side in the larger pot. Arrange the plants so that they will grow easily around the hoop, with the tallest shoots towards the outside. Top up with compost.

3 Insert the plastic-coated wire hoop, pushing the ends of the wire firmly into the compost as close to the stems of the young plants as possible.

4 Tie the shoots to the hoop with wire ties. They should be sufficiently pliable to be wound smoothly around the wire, which will help to keep the shape neat.

GARDENER'S TIP

Tie the young growth into the wire form every 2–3 days to ensure that the shape remains neat.

The pot should be turned completely every week, exposing both sides of the hoop to the light so that the growth is even.

A Hardy Fuchsia in a Border

A hardy fuchsia planted into a border will make a bright display of colour year after year. Established plants with a strong root system will produce flowers from early summer through to the autumn. 'Empress of Prussia', 'Hawkshead' and 'Army Nurse' are all hardy varieties that can tolerate temperatures of -5°C (23°F) or below.

MATERIALS AND TOOLS
Garden spade
Watering can

PLANTS
Hardy plant such as *Fuchsia* 'Empress of Prussia', 'Hawkshead' or 'Army Nurse'

hardy fuchsia

1 Using the spade, prepare the ground where you plan to plant the fuchsia. Clear away stones and debris. Plant in late spring, as soon as any danger of frost has passed.

2 Dig a hole larger and deeper than the pot holding the fuchsia. Heap the soil equally on both sides of the hole so that you can ease it back around the rootball when you have positioned the fuchsia.

3 Remove the plastic pot and position the plant in the hole. Ensure that the rootball sits below the level of the soil surface to reduce the danger of frost damage in subsequent winters.

4 Using the spade, push the soil back around the rootball. Gently firm or tread the soil around the freshly planted fuchsia, either with your hands or with your heel.

5 Water the plant and the surrounding soil area to ensure that no gaps remain around the roots.

GARDENER'S TIP

As an insurance against losing your plants through winter damage, take cuttings in early autumn and grow them in frost-free conditions. Use the tips of shoots produced on the mature growth as cutting material. Such cuttings will root easily and grow steadily through the winter. In the early summer, they will be suitable as replacement plants for any lost over the winter.

Fuchsia Hedge

Many people believe that hardy fuchsias are best displayed as hedging plants. They can grow naturally with the minimum of attention and will be a mass of colour all summer. Use plants of one variety only to ensure uniform growth. Fuchsia hedges are a vital part of the landscape of south-west Britain and the west coast of Ireland.

MATERIALS AND TOOLS
Measuring stick 30 cm (12 in) long
Spade
Chopped bark mulch

PLANTS
Hardy plant such as *Fuchsia magellanica* 'Riccartonii' and *F. magellanica* 'Tricolor'

hardy fuchsia

1 Set out the pots along the site prepared for the hedge. The distance between the plants is important, so use a measuring stick to space the plants approximately 30 cm (12 in) apart.

2 Dig a hole in the prepared ground twice as deep as the size of the fuchsia pot. The hole must be sufficiently deep for the top of the compost (soil mix) in the pot to be at least 6 cm (2¼ in) below the soil surface. This will prevent winter damage and encourage new shoots to grow from the base of the plant.

3 Remove the pot, set the rootball into the hole and cover with soil.

4 Spread the mulch of chopped bark over the soil surface in a layer approximately 5 cm (2 in) deep. This will suppress weeds and reduce moisture loss through evaporation.

GARDENER'S TIP

Soil preparation will determine the success of the hedge. The soil must be free-draining and at the same time not prone to drying out in spells of hot weather. Most soils can be improved for this purpose by adding organic matter in the form of garden compost (soil mix), leaf mould, chopped and partially rotted straw or spent mushroom compost (soil mix). It is advisable to start the preparation in the autumn, leaving the roughly dug soil exposed to winter frosts that will break down the larger clumps. Add the organic matter in the spring before you start to plant.

Foliage Hanging Basket

The attractive foliage of *Fuchsia* 'Autumnale' is shown to advantage in a hanging basket. The young leaves are green and yellow, maturing to dark red and salmon with splashes of yellow. Regular "stopping" of the growing tip will produce lots of brightly coloured new growth, which is used here to provide a contrast with green foliage in a conservatory.

MATERIALS AND TOOLS
Wire basket
Bucket
Sphagnum moss
Potting compost (soil mix)
Perlite
Watering can

PLANTS
Fuchsia 'Autumnale'

Fuchsia 'Autumnale'

1 To keep the basket stable while you work, place it on an empty bucket. Draw the hanging chain to one side.

2 Use small pads of moss to line the inside of the basket. Half-fill the basket with a lightweight, peat-free compost (soil mix). You can add perlite to the compost to decrease the weight.

3 Position the plants on the compost before removing their pots, to help you get the arrangement correct. Remove the pots before you plant each fuchsia.

4 Top up with compost so that the rootballs are well covered, and water the basket well to settle the compost before you hang it.

GARDENER'S TIP

F. 'Autumnale' has a horizontal growth habit, so it is most effective if grown in hanging baskets which are to be suspended at about eye level, or if it is used in the front of a mixed planting.

Mixed Foliage Wire Basket

Fuchsias are most often grown for their flowers, but there are many varieties that have lovely variegated leaves. A moss-lined decorative wire basket is an ideal way to present these foliage fuchsias. The moss lining will continue to look attractive as long as the basket is kept moist and in the light.

MATERIALS AND TOOLS
Wire basket
Sphagnum moss
Potting compost (soil mix)
Pelleted slow-release plant food granules
Watering can

PLANTS
Fuchsia 'Popsie Girl'
Fuchsia 'Cloth of Gold'
Fuchsia magellanica 'Alba Variegata'
3 sage
3 variegated ivies

Fuchsia *'Cloth of Gold'*

Fuchsia *'Popsie Girl'*

Fuchsia magellanica *'Alba Variegata'*

variegated ivy

sage

1 Line the basket with fresh, damp moss. If the moss has become dry and brittle, soak it overnight in water and then squeeze out the excess.

2 Use small clumps of moss rather than a few larger pieces. Push the moss firmly against the sides of the basket.

3 Fill the basket with compost (soil mix) and arrange the plants to make an attractive display, arranging the variegated ivy so that it trails over the side, and placing the sage plants between the fuchsias.

4 Add pellets of slow-release plant food granules to the basket and water the plants in.

GARDENER'S TIP

The fuchsias will grow well in the shade where the colour of their leaves is enhanced.

Standard Foliage Fuchsia

Fuchsia 'Tom West' is an excellent hardy variety that was first propagated in 1853. Underplanted with variegated ivy, and set off by the large Chinese-style glazed pot, this display has a very modern appeal.

MATERIALS AND TOOLS
Large glazed pot at least 70 cm (28 in) diameter
Crocks
Peat-free container compost (soil mix)
Slow-release plant food granules

PLANTS
Half-standard *Fuchsia* 'Tom West'
6 variegated ivy plants

variegated ivy

Fuchsia *'Tom West'*

1 Cover the drainage hole in the base of the pot with crocks. This prevents it becoming blocked and maintains the free drainage of excess water from the potting compost (soil mix).

2 Almost fill the pot with peat-free container compost, then add some slow-release plant food granules, following the manufacturer's instructions.

3 Remove the plastic pot from the fuchsia, and lower it gently on to the compost in the pot, positioning it so that the top of its rootball is slightly lower than the lip of the pot.

4 Add more compost around the fuchsia. Plant the variegated ivy plants around the base of the fuchsia. Fill in the gaps between the rootballs and gently tease the stems and foliage of the ivy across the compost surface. Water the arrangement.

GARDENER'S TIP

The variegated foliage of *Fuchsia* 'Tom West' develops a lovely rich pink colouring when grown in a sunny position. The best foliage colour is on the young growth, so regular pinching out will ensure a colourful plant.

Foliage Wall Pot

The bushy growth of *Fuchsia magellanica* 'Alba Variegata' is highly suited to displaying as a crown of leafy hair in a head-shaped wall pot. A classical head will add a timeless touch to a modern garden.

MATERIALS AND TOOLS
Classical head wall pot
Expanded clay granules

PLANTS
Fuchsia magellanica 'Alba Variegata'

Fuchsia magellanica
'Alba Variegata'

1 Check the wall pot for a hook or hanging point. The hanging point will need to be sufficiently strong to carry the weight of a moist plant pot.

2 Fill the wall pot with enough expanded clay granules to lift the top of the plant pot to the right level.

3 Place the fuchsia, still in its plant pot, in the wall pot.

4 Arrange the foliage to make a convincing leafy crown of hair for the head.

GARDENER'S TIP

Check the base of the wall pot for drainage holes. If there are no holes, you will need to remove the plant pot each time you water the fuchsia and allow the compost (soil mix) to drain before replacing it.

Fuchsias as Edging Plants

The golden-leaved *Fuchsia* 'Genii' makes a striking edging plant, either in a small garden where the bright foliage enhances a feature such as a curving bed, or in a larger garden where the bold colour of the leaves clearly marks the border.

Materials and Tools
Garden trowel

Plants
5 *Fuchsia* 'Genii' in 10 cm (4 in) pots for each 1 m (3 ft 4 in) of border

Fuchsia *'Genii'*

1 Position the plants along the edge of the bed where they are to be planted. Set the pots 20 cm (8 in) apart, to leave the fuchsias room to grow.

2 Using a trowel, dig a hole larger than the size of the fuchsia pot, loosening the soil at the base of the hole. This will encourage the fuchsia to root downwards. Remove the pot and check that the roots look healthy.

3 Plant the fuchsia in the hole. Ensure that the top of the potting compost (soil mix) is at least 3 cm (1¼ in) below the soil level. Use the trowel to push the soil back around the rootball.

4 Continue planting the fuchsias as they are positioned. Pinching out the tips of the shoots will encourage the plants to make full, compact bushes.

Gardener's Tip

Fuchsia 'Genii' will produce light yellow-green leaves on the reddish stems when grown in bright light, and more green leaves when grown in shade. Plants are super-hardy and can safely be left in position in most regions, with only a light protection of compost or mulch over the crowns.

Archway Planters

Setting paired planters on either side of an archway will frame the view and establish a focus on the arch. Elaborate planters provide sufficient detail to make a narrow archway exciting. Use herbs with scented leaves as the support plants. Their scent will be released as you walk by and brush against them.

MATERIALS AND TOOLS

- 2 x 45 cm (18 in) squares of hessian-backed (burlap-backed) carpet
- 2 galvanized iron-work planters 45 cm (18 in) diameter
- Fresh sphagnum moss
- 2 hessian (burlap) sacks
- Plastic pot
- Potting compost (soil mix)

PLANTS

- 2 standard *Fuchsia* 'Annabel'
- 4 *Petunia* 'Senator'
- 4 ivy-leaved pelargoniums
- 4 sage
- 4 curry plants
- 4 oregano

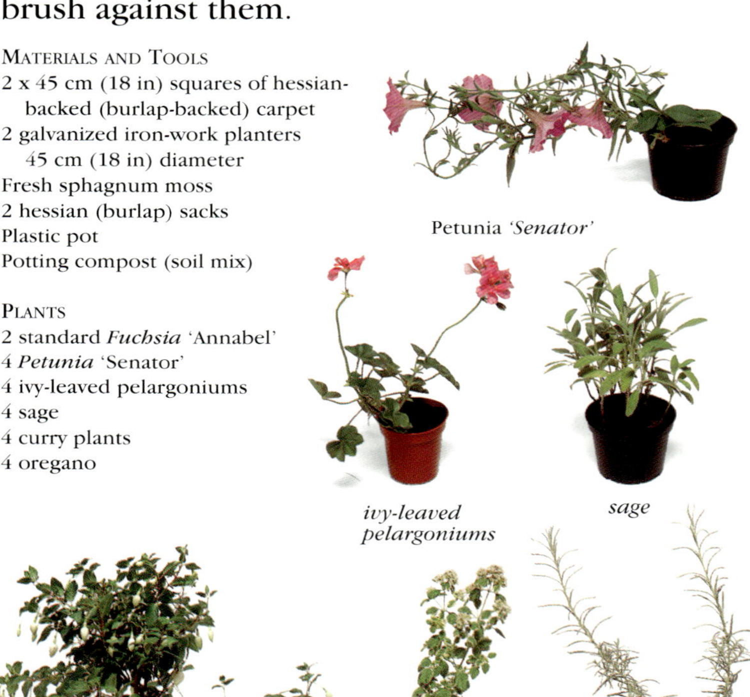

Petunia *'Senator'*

ivy-leaved pelargoniums

sage

curry plant

oregano

Fuchsia *'Annabel'*

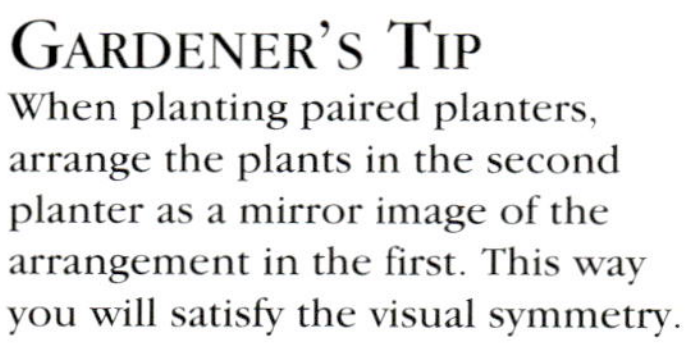

GARDENER'S TIP

When planting paired planters, arrange the plants in the second planter as a mirror image of the arrangement in the first. This way you will satisfy the visual symmetry.

1 Lay a square of carpet in the bottom of each planter. This will establish a firm base for the compost (soil mix). Starting at the bottom, press pads of fresh moss against the sides of the iron-work planter.

2 Place a hessian (burlap) sack in each planter, opening it wide to help hold the moss in place.

3 Using the plastic pot, start to fill the sack with compost. Push the compost into the corners of the sack to ensure that it spreads against the sides of the planter. As the sack is filled with compost, it will hold the moss against the sides of the planter.

4 Put more moss in place. Tuck in the top of the sack and finish putting moss against the sides of the planter to make a neat edge.

5 Plunge the standard fuchsia into the compost (soil mix).

6 Arrange the herbs and flowering plants around the base of the fuchsia.

Alpine Fuchsia in Copper

Some fuchsias are well suited to growing amongst a collection of alpine plants. They generally have small leaves and grow relatively slowly. Their woody growth can give height in a group of plants. The species most often used in this way is *Fuchsia microphylla*, a parent of the very delightful cultivar *Fuchsia* 'Lottie Hobby'.

MATERIALS AND TOOLS
Copper pan, alpine sink or other container
Drainage crocks
Gravel
Large stones
Gritty, soil-based compost (soil mix)

PLANTS
Alpine plants, including saxifrages and dianthus
Fuchsia 'Lottie Hobby'

Fuchsia *'Lottie Hobby'*

alpine plants

1 Check the depth of the container and the drainage potential. If the base has no holes, you will need to provide adequate drainage.

2 Lay crocks and gravel deeply across the base of the container. Aim to achieve an even layer of gravel, as an uneven surface will cause water to puddle and drainage material should be particularly deep here.

3 Place the large stones carefully. You should aim to create the impression that the stones are arising from under the soil or compost (soil mix), not sitting on its surface.

4 Fill the container with a gravel-rich compost. Soil-based compost will provide a suitable medium for most alpines as well as for the fuchsia plants.

5 Arrange the alpines and the fuchsia for maximum effect. Do this with the plastic pots still in place so you do not disturb the roots as you experiment with different positions.

6 Plant the fuchsia and the alpines, gently firming compost (soil mix) around the rootballs with your hands, and finally covering the surface of the compost with a gravel mulch that matches the large stones in colour and texture.

Gardener's Tip

The fuchsia will not be as hardy as the alpine plants, so plan your planting arrangement to enable you to lift the fuchsia for overwintering in frost-free conditions.

Courtyard Shell-planter

Any type of fuchsia can be grown in a patio planter, but upright growing plants with an erect habit are the most suitable for ground-level containers. Choose a cultivar that has flowers held horizontal and then match the supporting plants to your theme. The plants chosen here give the impression of sea spray and foam to match the shell planter.

MATERIALS AND TOOLS
Polystyrene blocks
Decorative planter
Potting compost (soil mix)
Horticultural-grade charcoal
Gravel for mulch

PLANTS
3 *Fuchsia* 'Gwen Dodge'
3 *Lotus berthelotii*
6 *Cineraria maritima*

Other suitable fuchsia cultivars are 'Army Nurse' or 'Cotton Candy'

Lotus berthelotii

Cineraria maritima

Fuchsia *'Gwen Dodge'*

1 Place some polystyrene blocks in the bottom of the planter to give good drainage and to reduce the eventual weight of the planter.

2 Fill the planter almost to the top with compost (soil mix). Add a sprinkling of horticultural-grade charcoal to keep the compost fresh.

GARDENER'S TIP

Regular removal of the dead flowers and young fruits from each fuchsia plant will ensure that flowers are continuously produced throughout the summer.

3 Position the plants while still in their pots, for ease of handling. Start with fuchsias as your main focus in the centre of the planter. Set the rootballs of the fuchsia plants close together, but slightly angled away from each other.

4 Add the grey foliage plants to create a soft edging to the planting group.

5 When satisfied, remove the plastic pots, plunge the plants into the compost (soil mix) and cover the rootballs with more compost.

6 Add a gravel mulch to the surface of the planter to prevent the compost drying out.

Colourful Patio Planters

Fuchsias are ideal for creating summer displays in containers. Where a courtyard or patio planter will be exposed to hot conditions, use one of the distinctive "triphylla" cultivars, which are able to cope with direct sun. The foliage is often dark or bronze and makes a striking display when mixed with variegated plants.

MATERIALS AND TOOLS
Crocks
Planter
Perlite
Peat-free container compost (soil mix)

PLANTS
Fuchsia 'Gartenmeister Bonstedt'
4 *Fuchsia* 'Nickis Findling'
2 variegated ivies

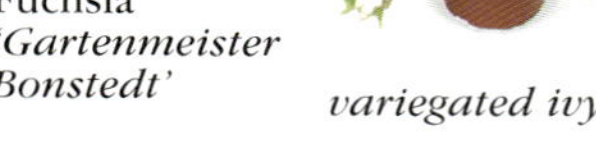

Fuchsia *'Gartenmeister Bonstedt'*

variegated ivy

1 Place crocks across the drainage hole of the planter and add a layer of perlite to help the drainage.

2 Fill the container almost to the top with a peat-free compost (soil mix) suitable for pots and containers.

GARDENER'S TIP

"Triphylla" cultivars are highly suitable for pots and tubs and will flower for months if kept neither too wet nor too dry. Remember to check the compost (soil mix) moisture by feeling it before you water. If the medium is too wet, the plants will lose their leaves.

3 Place *Fuchsia* 'Gartenmeister Bonstedt' centrally in the container.

4 Add the trailing foliage plants to either side of the front of the planter.

5 Position the supporting fuchsias at the centre front and around the back of the planter. Top up with compost and water the container.

Balcony Fuchsias

Many fuchsias produce graceful hanging branches and are highly suited to cultivating in balcony pots. The rich and complex shape of the flowers, especially the double forms, can be most fully appreciated when seen from below.

MATERIALS AND TOOLS
Plastic pots
Peat-free potting compost (soil mix)
Pelleted slow-release plant food granules
Checked terracotta pots
Drip irrigation system

PLANTS
5 *Fuchsia* 'Grandma Sinton'

1 Where roots are showing through the base of a pot, repot the fuchsia into a larger pot using a lightweight peat-free potting compost (soil mix).

Fuchsia *'Grandma Sinton'*

2 To maintain fertilizer levels, use fertilizer pellets that will release nutrients over the growing season. Place a single pellet in each pot, pushing it just below the surface of the compost.

3 Position a drip point near the centre of the pot, using the peg to hold the unit just above the surface of the compost. Arrange the fuchsias in decorative pots and adjust the irrigation system to reach each pot.

GARDENER'S TIP

Plants grown on balconies usually lose water at a high rate due to exposure to wind and sunshine. Watering is often a problem in these situations where access may be difficult and where drips and spills will wet people passing below. To avoid such spills and to ensure that your plants are well watered, use a drip irrigation system that will keep the potting compost (soil mix) moist. Each pot should be equipped with its own drip point, and the whole unit connected to a tap from which you control the flow.

Formal Fuchsia

To create a formal planting arrangement with fuchsias, use a single cultivar *en masse* rather than a mixture of different varieties. An interesting effect can be achieved using one of the cultivars with horizontal or even upright-growing flowers, which have more impact in a low-level container. Fill the container with fuchsias, or use them to surround a clipped bay tree for an impressive and elegant arrangement.

MATERIALS AND TOOLS
Planter
Crocks or polystyrene blocks
Potting compost (soil mix)

PLANTS
3 *Fuchsia* 'Pink Fantasia' or 'Rose Fantasia' or 'Diane Brown'
6 *Cineraria maritima*

Fuchsia *'Pink Fantasia'*

Cineraria maritima

1 Cover the base of the planter with a good depth of drainage material. A broken polystyrene plant tray is ideal.

2 Three-quarters fill the planter with compost (soil mix). Use a peat-free loam or organic-based compost (soil mix).

3 Position the plants while still in their plastic pots, to avoid damaging the roots. Arrange the plants symmetrically to create a formal design, placing the fuchsias in the centre and the cineraria down either side of the container.

4 Remove the plastic pots and top up with more compost. Water the container thoroughly.

GARDENER'S TIP

Beware of winter weather which will freeze the soil in the container. Remove the plants in autumn and replace them with hardy plants.

Bonsai Fuchsia

Almost all fuchsias can be grown as bonsai, since they are happy to be root-pruned. The most suitable fuchsias for bonsai have small leaves and small, delicate flowers. A plant that has started to become woody in its second growing season is ideal. If it has already developed an interesting form so much the better; if not, prune away some of the growth and wire the remaining branches into the desired positions.

Gardener's Tip

Never use a high-nitrogen fertilizer for a fuchsia bonsai. This would encourage the shoots to grow too weakly and rapidly. It is best to use an extra-dilute solution of a balanced feed, which will encourage both roots and shoots to grow at a reasonably slow rate.

Materials and Tools
Kitchen fork
Scissors or secateurs (pruners)
Small piece of fine netting
Gritty potting compost (soil mix) with added charcoal
Stick

Plants
Fuchsia 'String of Pearls' or 'Daisy Bell'

Fuchsia *'String of Pearls'*

1 Remove the plant from its pot and tease the compost (soil mix) from around the roots of the plant.

2 Using sharp scissors or secateurs (pruners), carefully cut away approximately two-thirds of the roots.

3 Cut away the top of the plastic pot to leave a small, low pot. Place fine netting across the drainage holes.

4 Repot the fuchsia, holding the plant upright and trickling charcoal-rich, gritty compost around the roots.

5 Gently firm the compost down, using a stick to ensure that all the spaces are filled. Water the fuchsia.

6 To encourage a "windswept" growth form, you can lay the plant on its side or at an angle for a couple of weeks.

Luxury Basket

***Fuchsia* 'Pink Galore' is a beautiful cultivar for a luxury hanging basket. The dark, glossy green foliage is a perfect foil for the full, soft rose-pink flowers. A plastic basket with a fixed reservoir has been used to facilitate growth and watering, and the curtains of stems will soon hide the basket.**

Gardener's Tip

Always use an odd number of plants to achieve the best effect. A plant placed centrally will prevent a gap appearing as the plants begin to cascade downwards.

Materials and Tools
Plastic hanging basket with fixed reservoir 36 cm (14 in) diameter
Peat-free potting compost (soil mix)
Slow-release plant food granules

Plants
5 *Fuchsia* 'Pink Galore'

Fuchsia *'Pink Galore'*

1 Check that the fibre wick is projecting downwards into the water reservoir. To avoid the plants becoming tangled in the chain, pull it to one side.

2 Put a layer of compost (soil mix), together with a measure of slow-release plant food granules, into the bottom of the hanging basket.

3 Arrange four of the plants in their pots around the edge of the basket in a symmetrical pattern. Place the last plant in the centre of the basket.

4 Remove the plastic pot from each fuchsia plant and gently seat the rootball into the compost.

5 Carefully fill the spaces between the pots with the mixed compost and fertilizer. Firm the compost with your hands to avoid leaving large spaces.

6 Tease the stems and the foliage around the chains as they are lifted into position for hanging.

Wedding Flowers

Fuchsia 'Happy Wedding Day' produces very large, round flowers. The lax growth makes it perfect for use in a decorative wire-work basket. As its name suggests, it is an ideal fuchsia to use as part of the decoration for a wedding display. Other white plants can be added to reinforce the impact of the fuchsia's fresh white flowers.

MATERIALS AND TOOLS
Sphagnum moss
Plastic pot
Garden twine
Green bin (sheet) moss
Wirework basket

PLANTS
3 *Fuchsia* 'Happy Wedding Day'
3 *Fuchsia* 'Annabel' or 'Igloo Maid'
3 busy lizzies
3 white lace-cap hydrangea

Fuchsia *'Happy Wedding Day'*

GARDENER'S TIP

To ensure that you have a strong display with lots of flowers, remember that you will need to cease "stopping" the plants at least 8 weeks in advance. This way there will be sufficient time for the flowers to develop on the young growth.

1 Make a hand-sized pad of fresh moss and start to cover the plastic pot.

2 Use one end of a long piece of twine to tie the moss in place. Leave the other end loose.

3 Work around the pot, adding small pads of moss and using the end of the twine to secure them. The twine will be hidden in the soft form of the moss.

4 When the pot is covered, add a further layer of green bin (sheet) moss and insert it in a wirework basket. Group the fuchsias and other plants in a suitable container for a lovely display.

Fire and Earth

The earth tones of this small decorative terracotta window box are topped with the fiery reds and oranges of the plants – the fuchsia with its bronze foliage and tubular scarlet flowers, the orange nasturtiums and the red, claw-like flowers of the feathery-leaved lotus.

Materials and Tools
Terracotta window box 36 cm (14 in) long
Crocks or other drainage material
Potting compost (soil mix)
Slow-release plant food granules
Watering can

Plants
Fuchsia 'Thalia'
3 orange nasturtiums 'Empress of India' or similar
2 *Lotus berthelotti*

nasturtiums 'Empress of India'

Lotus berthelotti

Fuchsia *'Thalia'*

Gardener's Tip

Prevent the nasturtiums from becoming "leggy" by pinching out the growing tips frequently.

1 Cover the base of the window box with drainage material.

2 Fill in the window box with compost (soil mix), mixing in a teaspoon of slow-release plant food granules. Plant the fuchsia in the centre of the window box.

3 Position and plant the three nasturtiums, evenly spaced, along the back of the window box.

4 Plant the two lotuses in the front of the window box on either side of the fuchsia. Water thoroughly, leave to drain, and stand in a sunny position.

Edible Half-basket

It is always great fun to be able to eat what you grow, and this half-basket combines two small fruits. *Fuchsia procumbens,* a trailing species from New Zealand, produces fruits the size of a miniature damson plum and they grow well with the delicate fruits of the alpine strawberry.

MATERIALS AND TOOLS
Wire half-basket
Bucket
Cardboard liner
Peat-free compost (soil mix)
Slow-release plant food granules
Watering can

PLANTS
3 alpine strawberries
3 *Fuchsia procumbens*

alpine strawberry

Fuchsia procumbens

1 With the half-basket placed on the bucket for stability, position the cardboard liner to fit inside it.

2 Fill the half-basket with peat-free compost (soil mix).

3 Add slow-release plant food granules to the compost. Follow the directions on the package for the correct dosage for a half-basket.

4 Position the plants in the basket before removing their pots, to help you get the arrangement correct.

5 When you are happy with the arrangement, remove each plastic pot and cover the rootballs with compost.

6 Water the basket to settle the compost around the rootballs of the plants. Try to press the stems of the fuchsias into the compost, along their complete length. They will produce roots easily and encourage the rapid growth of the plants.

GARDENER'S TIP

This combination of plants is suitable for a shady position. *Fuchsia procumbens* is a wonderful ground-cover plant and is hardy except in the harshest winters. A layer of leaves or straw will protect it from extreme cold.

Fuchsia Wall Pot

While you may not want to have a water feature in your garden, a terracotta wall fountain can still make a lovely planting pot. *Fuchsia* 'Daisy Bell' is a good example of a cultivar that is particularly suited to growing in hanging baskets. Its growth is trailing, lax and self-branching, and it produces numerous flowers freely throughout the summer.

1 Prop the wall fountain upright securely using the bricks. Make sure that the planting bowl is held straight, so that you can create a balanced arrangment.

2 Pour a couple of potfuls of the expanded clay granules into the container to ensure good aeration and drainage at the base of the planting bowl.

MATERIALS AND TOOLS
Terracotta wall fountain
Bricks
Expanded clay granules
Peat-free potting compost (soil mix)
Water-retaining gel (optional)

PLANTS
3 *Fuchsia* 'Daisy Bell'

Fuchsia *'Daisy Bell'*

3 Fill the planting bowl with a peat-free compost (soil mix). Add a water-retaining gel to this if you wish.

4 Arrange the plants while still in their pots. Remove the pots and plant the fuchsias, adding extra compost to cover the rootballs.

5 Add a layer of clay granules on top of the compost as a mulch to prevent excessive water loss through evaporation.

GARDENER'S TIP

Avoid using a fuchsia cultivar that needs regular "stopping" to encourage branching for a wall-pot planting. You can reduce the maintenance of such a wall pot by using a fuchsia that is self-branching, such as 'Daisy Bell'.

Festive Fuchsias

Giving plants as gifts has been a custom since time immemorial. Fuchsia plants in full flower make wonderful gifts and, due to the ease with which they can be grown and propagated, you can be sure that your gift will go on bringing pleasure. *Fuchsia* 'Alice Hoffman' makes a wonderful gift for a novice plantsman. It is a hardy fuchsia that will flower easily and remain in good condition throughout the season.

MATERIALS AND TOOLS
Leaf shine spray
Expanded clay granules
Wrapping paper

PLANTS
Fuchsia 'Alice Hoffman'

Fuchsia *'Alice Hoffman'*

GARDENER'S TIP

Only use leaf shine on smooth-leaved plants. It will burn leaves that are soft and velvety in texture. Never spray plants that are located in direct sunlight or those that are wilted through water stress.

1 Remove all dead or yellowing leaves. Check the plant for old flowers or fruits as these will reduce the maintenance of continuous flower production.

2 Ensure the plant is well watered. Spray the foliage with leaf shine, which will remove all traces of lime.

3 Cover the compost (soil mix) surface with expanded clay granules. Wrap the pot in festive wrapping paper.

Contrasting Fuchsias

The strong colours of fuchsia flowers can be dramatically offset with painted terracotta pots. The exaggerated shape of the Long Tom pot matches the very long flowers of the "triphylla" group, *Fuchsia* 'Trumpeter'.

Materials and Tools
Paintbrush
Paint-mixing container
Mediterranean-blue emulsion paint
Terracotta Long Tom pot 30 cm (12 in) diameter
Crocks, polystyrene or other drainage material
Potting compost (soil mix)

Plants
Fuchsia 'Trumpeter'

Fuchsia *'Trumpeter'*

1 Paint the pot with the emulsion paint. To obtain a strong vibrant colour, it may be necessary to apply two coats. The terracotta will absorb the moisture from the paint so the pot will dry quickly.

2 Put the drainage material into the bottom of the Long Tom. The great depth of this pot is not necessary for the growth of the fuchsia, so it is possible to use drainage material to a depth of 15 cm (6 in).

3 Remove the plant from its plastic pot and repot it into the painted Long Tom so that the surface of the rootball is well below the rim of the pot.

4 Ease compost (soil mix) around the rootball, ensuring that it is really well covered and the plant is securely bedded into the compost.

Gardener's Tip

Plant *Fuchsia* 'Bealings' in a green pot to reinforce the contrasting image. The purple flowers of this fuchsia will contrast well with bright green and also with the *Fuchsia* 'Trumpeter's' flowers.

A Daring Window Box

The colour of the fuchsia flowers is echoed by the deep purple and crimson petunias in this window box, which also includes trailing campanula and catmint.

Materials and Tools

76 cm (30 in) plastic window box
90 cm (3 ft) wooden window box (optional)
Potting compost (soil mix)
Slow-release plant food granules

Plants

Fuchsia 'Dollar Princess'
2 low-growing catmint *(Nepeta mussinii)*
2 white-flowered *Campanula isophylla*
2 crimson petunias
2 purple petunias

Campanula isophylla

Nepeta mussinii

crimson petunia

purple petunia

Fuchsia *'Dollar Princess'*

1 Check the drainage holes are open in the base and, if not, drill or punch them open. Fill the box with compost (soil mix), mixing in 3 teaspoons of slow-release plant food granules. Plant the fuchsia in the centre of the window box.

2 Plant the catmint at either end of the window box.

3 Plant the campanula next to the catmint.

4 Plant the crimson petunias on either side of the fuchsia at the back of the window box.

5 Plant the purple petunias on either side of the fuchsia at the front of the window box. Water thoroughly and allow to drain.

6 Lower the plastic window box into place inside the wooden window box, if using. Stand in a sunny position.

Flower Tower

A hanging garden can be created using a flower tower with a suspended reservoir. Use plants of a single fuchsia cultivar for maximum impact, or several different cultivars for a softer effect.

MATERIALS AND TOOLS
Flower tower
Plastic pot
Lightweight peat-free potting compost (soil mix)
Scissors or sharp knife
Watering can

PLANTS
15 *Fuchsia* 'Eva Boerg'

Fuchsia *'Eva Boerg'*

1 Place the flower tower on a firm surface and arrange the chain to one side of the plastic tube. Using the plastic pot, fill the flower tower with lightweight potting compost (soil mix).

2 Do not tamp the compost down firmly, but make sure that the tower is filled out to its full width and height. It should be self-supporting when filled. Using the marked positions printed on the tower, make a cross-cut through the outer plastic sheath and through the inner netting tube with a pair of scissors or a sharp knife.

3 Open the slit fully. Each slit should be just long enough for you to be able to insert the rootball of the plant through the hole.

4 Take a plant from its pot and push the rootball into the compost through the hole in both the plastic tube and the inner net. Gently gather the compost around the rootball so that it is bedded in but not squashed or damaged. Angle the stem upwards slightly so that the plant can grow easily.

5 When planting is complete, top up the tower with compost if necessary. Water the tower by pouring about 1 litre (1¾ pints) of water into the top of the tower. It will filter down slowly and settle the compost around the newly positioned plants. After the initial top watering, water the tower by filling the reservoir at the bottom.

GARDENER'S TIP

Take care not to overwater the flower tower, which will hold a good amount of water in the compost (soil mix). This is particularly important in the first weeks after planting, while the young plants are becoming established.

Fuchsias for Tots

Several fuchsia cultivars are excellent plants for children to grow, particularly 'Happy' and 'Tom Thumb'. These fuchsias can be purchased at the start of the summer in small pots or polystyrene trays. Transferred to brightly painted pots on a windowsill or in a light corner of the children's room, they will produce flowers continuously throughout the summer.

MATERIALS AND TOOLS
Small terracotta pots 8 cm (3¼ in) diameter
Acrylic or craft paints
Paintbrush
Masking tape
Crocks
Potting compost (soil mix)
Slow-release plant food granules

PLANTS
Dwarf fuchsias

dwarf fuchsia

1 Paint the pots with bright primary colours in stripes or bold patterns. To paint careful geometric patterns, use masking tape to mask out specific areas. Let the paint dry before you continue.

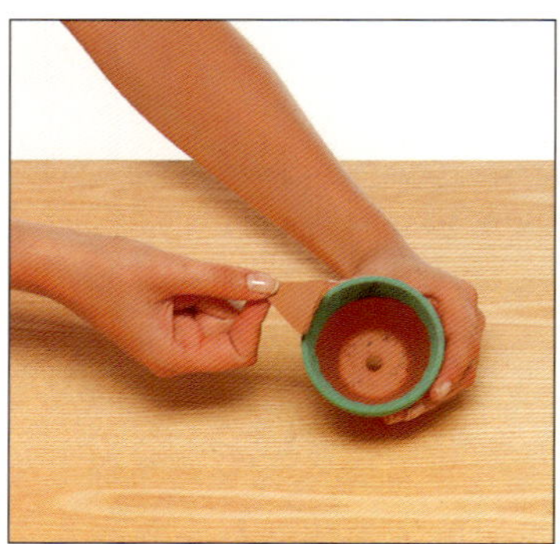

2 Place small crocks or pieces of polystyrene in the bottom of the pots to cover the drainage hole.

3 Remove the fuchsias from their plastic pots and place one plant in each terracotta pot. Top up with potting compost (soil mix) that has been mixed with slow-release plant food granules.

4 Use the blunt end of the paintbrush to ease the compost into the narrow gap between the plant's rootball and the pot. Tamp the compost firmly but not too tightly. Water the pots and allow them to drain.

Miniature Fuchsias

A square terracotta tray makes a suitable container for growing a mass of miniature fuchsias. A mixture of two varieties with different coloured foliage will give an interesting checkered effect to the planting.

Materials and Tools
Terracotta tray 30 cm (12 in) square
Crocks
Potting compost (soil mix)

Plants
4 *Fuchsia* 'Elf'
4 *Fuchsia* 'Red Imp'

Fuchsia *'Elf'*

Fuchsia *'Red Imp'*

1 Cover the drainage holes in the bottom of the tray with crocks. Put some compost (soil mix) into the tray to a depth of approximately 13 cm (5 in).

2 Arrange the plants in an alternating pattern in the tray.

3 When you are happy with the arrangement of plants, remove the fuchsias from the plastic pots and plant them in the compost.

4 Fill the gaps between the rootballs with compost, easing it into place and pressing it firmly around the rootballs.

Gardener's Tip

Both these cultivars are hardy, but when grown in a pot the arrangement will need frost protection because the soil will freeze around their roots.

Tropical Fuchsias

Some cultivars require careful treatment, especially with regard to watering and growing conditions. One such fuchsia is 'Major Heaphy', which produces flowers continuously, but can drop all these and the buds too if the atmosphere becomes too dry. One way of displaying these fuchsias is to create a tropical corner using other plants that also need high humidity. Grow them in a warm, sheltered place where you can build up a humid atmosphere.

GARDENER'S TIP

For a perfect finishing touch to create a really tropical look, why not try placing plenty of straw or raffia around the plants on top of the compost (soil mix).

MATERIALS AND TOOLS
Large bowl
Hessian (burlap) sack
Expanded clay granules
A few handfuls of straw (optional)

PLANTS
Standard *Fuchsia* 'Major Heaphy'
Abutilon

Abutilon

Fuchsia *'Major Heaphy'*

1 Place the bowl inside the sack. This will form the base of the display and enable you to water the plants carefully.

2 Put a layer of expanded clay granules into the bowl. These granules hold water which, as it slowly evaporates, will increase the humidity in the atmosphere.

3 Position the standard fuchsia centrally in the bowl.

4 Position the abutilon in the bowl around the central standard fuchsia.

5 Draw the sack up around the base of all the plants to create the impression that they are a single unit.

Fuchsia Tube

A purpose-designed plastic tube with pre-cut planting holes offers a great solution to creating a hanging display. Mixing flowering and foliage plants in containers can be very satisfactory, as the foliage plants will provide interest and colour before the flowering plants get started.

MATERIALS AND TOOLS
Perlite
Potting compost (soil mix)
Water-retaining gel
Plastic pot
Plastic tube

PLANTS
Fuchsia 'Squadron Leader' or 'Hazel'

Fuchsia *'Squadron Leader'*

GARDENER'S TIP

Regular feeding and watering is vital to maintain balanced growth. Use young, healthy plants, and remember that you should combine plants that have similar rates and forms of growth so that one does not swamp the other.

1 Mix the perlite into the compost (soil mix), adding about one part perlite to two parts compost. Add water-retaining gel following the manufacturer's instructions.

2 Using a plastic pot, start to fill the plastic tube with the compost mixture. Fill the tube to the depth of the first planting holes.

3 Push the rootballs of the young plants through the cut planting positions. Angle the plant slightly upwards, so that it does not slip out of the hole before it can become established.

4 Add compost to cover the first rootballs and continue placing the young plants up the tube. Do not cut extra holes in the tube, as this would pack the plants too tightly. The small plants you start with will need space to grow.

5 Firm the compost down over the rootballs as you move up the tube, to avoid leaving any gaps in the column of compost. The tube should stand unsupported as you near the top of the planting.

6 When the last planting positions are filled, top up the tube with compost. Tamp it into the tube but do not push too hard; the aim is to create a firm column of compost.

Fuchsia Bricks

A simple engineering brick holding three miniature fuchsias can make a delightful arrangment for a special gift, or you could use it as a doorstop or windowsill decoration. Start the project with young plants, either grown from cuttings or purchased early in the year from a good nursery.

Materials and Tools
Squares of wire mesh
Engineering brick
Potting compost (soil mix)
Pencil or cane

Plants
3 *Fuchsia* 'Tom Thumb'

Other suitable fuchsia cultivars are 'Son of Thumb', 'Lady Thumb', 'Tinker Bell'

Fuchsia *'Tom Thumb'*

1 Bend the wire mesh and push it down into each hole, to form a cup-like base. The jagged edges of the wire should hold it firmly in position.

2 Remove the fuchsia plants from their pots, and fit one plant into each of the holes in the brick.

3 Ease compost (soil mix) around each plant, filling the hole completely. Use a pencil or cane to tamp the compost gently around the rootball of the small plant.

Gardener's Tip

To water your brick, immerse it completely in a basin of water at least twice a week. If the compost (soil mix) is allowed to dry out it will be very difficult to re-wet it completely.

Traditional Fuchsia

***Fuchsia* 'Thalia' was bred in 1905, in Germany. It is one of the most popular and easy "triphylla" cultivars to grow, and thrives in a large pot.**

Materials and Tools
Old handmade terracotta pot
Bucket of water
Crock
Peat-free compost (soil mix)

Plants
Fuchsia 'Thalia'

Fuchsia *'Thalia'*

1 Water your plant well by plunging the entire pot in a bucket before repotting. Wait for the compost (soil mix) to stop releasing air bubbles before you take it out. If you put a dry rootball into fresh compost it will never become properly moistened and the plant will suffer water stress.

2 Choose a terracotta pot that is just slightly larger than the existing pot and plunge and soak it before use. Terracotta will soak up enormous amounts of water and if the pot is dry, water will be absorbed from the fresh compost.

3 Use a crock at the base of the pot to cover the hole and prevent it becoming blocked with compost.

4 Repot the fuchsia, packing the compost around the rootball.

Gardener's Tip

This fuchsia grows into a strong bush if you pinch out the growing tips early in the season.

Bedding Fuchsias

Bedding fuchsias are usually sold as plantlets in modules. For the best display you need to plant them early in the season to allow them to develop fully. If you cannot plant until late spring or early summer, because of late frosts, either pot up the plantlets and grow them on under glass or buy pot-grown plants later on.

MATERIALS AND TOOLS
Fork
Rake
Wooden board
Cloche

PLANTS
Bedding fuchsias such as 'Estelle Marie', 'Koralle', 'Margaret Roe', 'Nellie Nuttall' or 'Thalia'

young plants

1 Fork over the site to break up the soil; remove any weeds, using a hand fork, and finally rake over the soil to level it.

2 Use a straight edge to mark the positions of the plants. Space them evenly – 20–38 cm (8 in – 1¼ ft). Check their ultimate size – at their peak they should touch, but not restrict each other's growth.

3 Plant the fuchsias and firm them in with your fingers.

4 Water in well. Once planted, water the fuchsias frequently, particularly in times of drought, and provide a liquid feed as for pot plants.

5 If a late frost is threatened, protect the plants with a cloche. The top half of a clear plastic drinks bottle, with the cap removed to allow for air circulation, makes a good improvised cloche for small plants.

GARDENER'S TIP

You can sink container-grown fuchsias directly into the soil in their pots. This may even accelerate and improve flowering, since the roots are restricted, but you will need to water and feed more frequently during the summer.

Woven Sheep Feeder

A woven willow sheep-feeder brimming with leaves creates an unusual feature on a lawn or a terrace. In Victorian times baskets would be placed to highlight particular garden features and filled with colourful and scented summer bedding plants.

MATERIALS AND TOOLS
- Willow sheep-feeder basket, approximately 1 m (3 ft 4 in) diameter
- Wooden mallet
- Old, hessian-backed (burlap-backed) carpet
- Polystyrene blocks for drainage
- Loam-based potting compost (soil mix)
- Watering can

PLANTS
- Standard *Fuchsia* 'Annabel'
- 3 bush *Fuchsia* 'Dark Eyes'
- 6 busy lizzies
- 6 *Cineraria maritima*
- 3 variegated ivies
- 3 *Petunia* 'Senator'
- 3 ivy-leaved pelargoniums

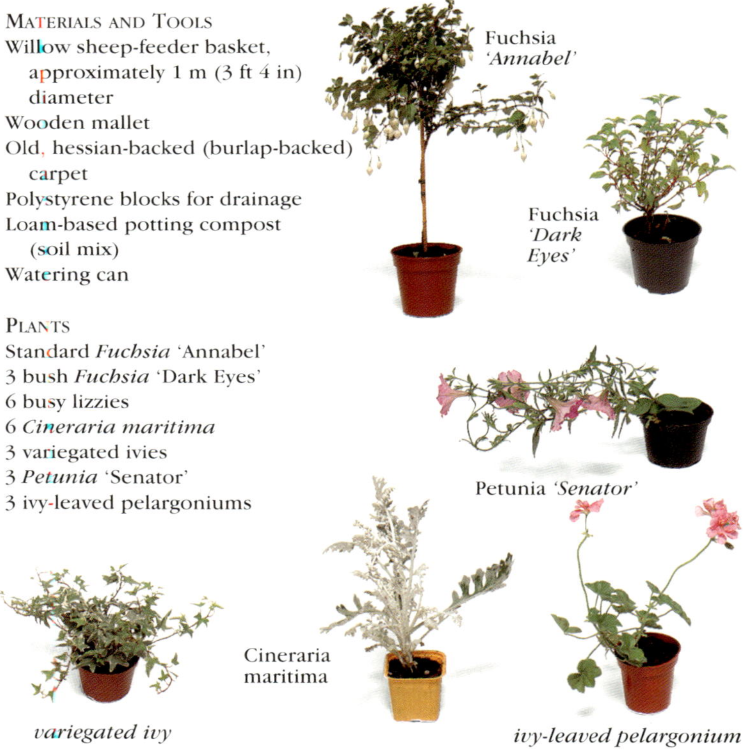

GARDENER'S TIP

Strong woven willow structures are semi-permanent and will be sufficiently hardy to withstand most winter weather. The soil mass within the structure will probably freeze during the coldest winter months, so beware: you will risk losing any plants that remain in the soil.

1 Position the basket on a flat lawn or terrace. Use a wooden mallet to hammer the sharp ends of the upright willow poles into place in the ground.

2 Line the sides of the basket with the carpet. Place the hessian side outermost, so that any colours in the carpet are hidden against the soil.

3 Break up the polystyrene and place in the base of the basket. Fill the basket with loam-based potting compost (soil mix).

4 Position the plants while they are still in their pots. Place the focal fuchsia plants first. Put the standard plant in the centre of the planting. This will give height to the display and will balance the arrangement.

5 Fill the remaining spaces with the support plants that you have chosen for the display. Once you are happy, remove the plastic pots and plunge the rootballs into the compost (soil mix).

6 Add compost to the planting so that all the rootballs are well covered. Do not tamp the compost down; it will find its own level when you water for the first time. You may need to add extra compost after this first watering.

Period Fuchsias

Fuchsias were first introduced to cultivation in Europe in the 1780s. Many cultivars that were bred in the 1800s can still be found in cultivation today. *Fuchsia* 'Bland's New Striped' was first seen in cultivation in 1872, and *Fuchsia* 'Claire de Lune' in 1880. Growing such plants that originated during a particular period will add an exciting detail to any collection.

Gardener's Tip

Orange flowers are often considered to be a modern advance in fuchsia cultivars, but 'Lye's Unique' has salmon-orange flowers and arose in 1886. Another old variety to look out for is 'Charming', a hardy bush that was developed in 1877.

Materials and Tools

Expanded clay granules
Victorian copper pot
Victorian style planter
Crocks
Peat-free container compost (soil mix)

Plants

Fuchsia 'Claire de Lune'

Fuchsia *'Bland's New Striped'*

Fuchsia *'Claire de Lune'*

1 Put a layer of expanded clay granules into the base of the pot. This will help to maintain a humid atmosphere as water evaporates from them.

2 Place the *Fuchsia* 'Claire de Lune' in the copper pot, arranging the branches and foliage to fall around the sides.

3 Cover the drainage hole in the bottom of the Victorian-style planter with crocks.

4 Part-fill the pot with compost (soil mix).

5 Remove the pot from the *Fuchsia* 'Bland's New Striped' . The visible network of fresh, healthy roots shows that the plant is strong and vigorous.

6 Transfer it into the planter. Cover the rootball and firm the compost with your hands.

Smelting Pot Fuchsias

The tall and elegant form of this antique smelting pot is well suited as a container for *Fuchsia* 'Kolding Perle'. This cultivar grows strongly and is dependable for a stunning display of flowers.

GARDENER'S TIP

Be very careful not to overwater a container like this which has no drainage holes.

MATERIALS AND TOOLS

- Broken polystyrene blocks for drainage
- Smelting pot or other tall planter 60 cm (24 in) high
- Plastic pot
- Expanded clay granules
- Container compost (soil mix)
- Watering can

PLANTS

- *Fuchsia* 'Kolding Perle' or 'Lye's Unique'
- 4 *Helichrysum argentium* or *H. petiolare*

Fuchsia *'Kolding Perle'*

Helichrysum argentium

1 Put the drainage material into the bottom of the smelting pot to a depth of 10 cm (4 in).

2 Using the plastic pot, pour expanded clay granules over and around the polystyrene to a depth of 30 cm (12 in).

3 Fill the smelting pot with container compost (soil mix) to approximately 20 cm (8 in) below the top of the pot.

4 Position the plants, starting with the fuchsia and placing the *Helichrysum* around its base.

5 Remove the plastic pots before planting each plant.

6 Fill between the plants with compost, pressing down firmly so that no air gaps are left around the roots. Water the container and place in a sunny position.

Index

Acknowledgements

Many thanks to the following nurseries for supplying plants and shoot locations:

Anglia Alpines, St Ives Road, Somersham, Huntingdon, Cambs PE17 3ET

Clifton Nurseries, Clifton Villas, Little Venice, London W9 2PX

Clay Lane Nursery, 3 Clay Lane, South Nutfield, Surrey RH1 4EG

Little Brook Fuchsias, Ash Green Lane West, Ash Green, Aldershot, Hampshire GU12 6HL